Once upon a time, there was a place called And.
It had the longest sentences in all the land.

Every sentence was such a drama—
that is, until folks met the comma.

As soon as Comma came to town,
he took their sentences and cut them down.

Before that, lists went on and on—
and conversations made folks yawn!

But with Comma around, it was easily seen,

you could take out the *ands* and put commas between.

Next, Comma showed what he could do
when perched beside an adjective or two.

On a separate sheet, shorten this sentence by replacing all but the last *and* with commas:

The kitten was small and furry and mischievous and playful and cuddly.

With Comma's help, their sign looked neater—
crisper, cleaner, shorter, and sweeter!

Yet there was more that Comma could do.
He cleaned up confusing sentences, too:
As Sue sat down to eat her dog took a bite!
Sue ATE her dog?! That couldn't be right.

> As Sue sat down to eat, her dog took a bite.

After

CHOMP!

DOG TALES

Where do you think commas should go in this sentence?

Just before bed he took a bubble bath read a book and drank hot chocolate.

Do not panic! Do not fear!
One little comma makes it all clear:
As Sue sat down to eat, her dog took a bite.
He bit her burger? Now that sounds right!

What's more, just by adding some curlicue dots,

Comma can join up two separate thoughts!

Instead of two sentences:

My fish is red. His name is Ned.

11

There can be just one:
Ned, my fish, is red.

On a separate sheet of paper, shorten the sentence by replacing all but the last *and* with commas.

We went on the Stupendo Slide and then we went on the Gigantor Swings and then we went on the Turbo Wheel and then we went on the Glow-Coaster!

Everything was easier to understand
when Comma came to the land of And!

But then, one day, with a great big sigh,
it was time for Comma to say good-bye.

There were other places he needed to go—
like But and Yet, not to mention Although.

Commas can often be found in sentences that have the words *but*, *yet*, and *although*. See if you can figure out where commas belong in these sentences:

1. She loves soccer but not as much as gymnastics.

2. He tried and tried yet he just couldn't hula-hoop.

3. I don't like broccoli although I do prefer it to asparagus.

The folks of And would miss Comma a lot.
Still, they'd never forget the lessons he taught.

"Safe trip! Thank you!" everyone cheered.

"We've learned so much since you've been here!"